C000148479

LOST COUNTRY HOUSES
of KENT

MARTIN EASDOWN

AMBERLEY

A country house lost to suburbia: Camps Hill, Lewisham, demolished in 1947.

To my father, Victor, a steadfast and proud supporter of my writing.

First published 2017

Amberley Publishing
The Hill, Stroud, Gloucestershire, GL5 4EP
www.amberley-books.com

Copyright © Martin Easdown, 2017

The right of Martin Easdown to be identified as the
Author of this work has been asserted in accordance with
the Copyrights, Designs and Patents Act 1988.

ISBN 978 1 4456 7434 6 (print)
ISBN 978 1 4456 7435 3 (ebook)

All rights reserved. No part of this book may be reprinted
or reproduced or utilised in any form or by any electronic,
mechanical or other means, now known or hereafter
invented, including photocopying and recording, or in
any information storage or retrieval system, without the
permission in writing from the Publishers.

British Library Cataloguing in Publication Data.
A catalogue record for this book is available from the
British Library.

Origination by Amberley Publishing.
Printed in Great Britain.

CONTENTS

Lees Court, Sheldwich, on fire, 20 November 1910.

Preston Hall, Aylesford – Demolished in 1848 and Replaced by a New House

Throughout the centuries many of Kent's great houses were enlarged and modernised, and in some cases totally rebuilt. We will see some of these in the final chapter of this book, but here we see the original houses of what became two eminent Kent institutions. Preston Hall was owned by the famous Kentish family the Culpeppers from c. 1300–1734, and the house seen above was rebuilt in the 1770s. It was demolished in 1848 by railway contractor Edward Ladd Betts and replaced by a sumptuous (but not universally liked) Jacobean mansion, which was later used by the British Legion as a TB hospital. Hemsted Park was a large Elizabethan mansion, which was subsequently reduced in size before it was demolished in 1860 and replaced by a new house in an Elizabethan style. Since 1923 this has been home to the famous Benenden School – a private girls' boarding school – where Princess Anne was a pupil.

Hemsted Park, Benenden – Demolished in 1860 and Replaced by a New House

HEMSTED, KENT, IN THE TIME OF THE GULDEFORDS.

INTRODUCTION

The country house and its estate is one of England's most enduring picturesque images. A grand historical mansion, surrounded by beautiful gardens and parkland with associated farms, cottages, and villages, seems the very epitome of England's green and pleasant land. And the county of Kent, affectionately known as the 'Garden of England', boasts of some fine country houses, which include Broome Park, Chevening, Cobham Hall, Knole, Leeds Castle, Mereworth Castle, and Penshurst Place. But, as elsewhere in the country, Kent has also lost its fair share of grand houses.

This book is the first to document the lost country houses of Kent (I have also included the Metropolitan Kent area), and I feel I have included all of the main houses since the eighteenth century that have been demolished, partially demolished, or rebuilt following a fire. However, it would require a larger volume than this to document every large house that has disappeared in Kent. I have included what are normally thought of as country houses, but have omitted manor houses, which were often replaced by country houses from the seventeenth century onwards. Castles (which have been well documented in print) have generally been left out, although those that did evolve into country houses and then were subsequently demolished – such as Scotney and Sissinghurst – have been included. Hadlow Castle, though, was never a castle, nor was Kearsney Abbey an abbey. Lost seaside villas, such as Encombe and Enbrook in Sandgate, which could be thought of as smaller country houses by the sea, have also not been included.

During their principal development between the seventeenth and nineteenth centuries, country houses became the showpieces of the nation's elite, who were the basis of political power after assuming the role of government from the Crown. An owner's desire to improve the standard of their living accommodation and keep up with the latest fashions in architecture led to existing houses being enlarged, or to some being abandoned or demolished to enable a grander and more modern residence to be built. Other losses during the eighteenth and nineteenth centuries were due to owners who held at least two houses, demolishing one of them to concentrate on the other. These new and larger country houses became communities in their own right, with a sizable amount of staff overseeing not only the house but the attached pleasure gardens, farms, stables, kitchen garden, workshops, icehouse, dairy, laundry, and kennels. The country house and its estate not only provided income for its owner, but employment for the locals. Granted, the wages were lower than in manufacturing jobs, but estate staff were often provided with free housing and rates. The 'big house' provided patronage and funds to the village church and school, and was often looked upon with a certain amount of pride by the villagers. They viewed the pleasure gardens with wonderment, which were usually fashioned by the eighteenth-century landscape movement that took the gentry by storm. Professional landscape gardeners, such as Lancelot 'Capability' Brown (1716–83) and Humphry Repton (1752–1818), were engaged to transform the grounds of country houses with eye-catching additions such as Gothic temples, towers, obelisks, grottos, and caves.

However, by the end of the nineteenth century, dark clouds were looming on the horizon for some country houses and their owners: the introduction of death duties in 1894 dealt a severe financial blow to landowners, and the new twentieth century brought increased taxation. Some owners began contemplating freeing themselves of not only the expense of a large house, but also the trappings of wealth and redundant privilege that the house and estate represented. Personal incompetence and extravagance, individual whims and fancies, and the extinction of landowning families also played their part in the loss of the country house. Yet it was the period between the two world wars that saw an acceleration in their demise. Death duties and taxation continued to rise, and some houses were let out to wealthy tenants with aspirations to live in such a grand abode. This ultimately proved to be an unreliable solution, and the houses, which frankly had become too big to live in, were demolished and their estates sold off – in some cases for property development in the face of relentless urbanisation. By the 1920s social change and economic decline dictated that the cheap servant economy the house owners depended on was in short supply due to a shortage of labour left by the First World War, and a consequent rise in wages. The Second World War struck a mortal blow to some houses. Many were requisitioned by the military, who left them in such a deplorable state that post-war compensation did not cover the cost of restoration. Fire often finished them off. The 1950s saw the peak of country house destruction, not only in Kent (where twenty-three perished) but all over the United Kingdom, where, in 1955, a country house was demolished every five days.

Fortunately, by the late 1960s the destruction of country houses had been reduced to a trickle, aided by the passing of the Town and Country Planning Act 1968, which compelled owners to seek and then wait for permission to demolish a building. The Act also gave local authorities powers to protect and spot list a building.

Since 1900, 1,200 country houses have been demolished in England – accounting for one in six of them. However, despite these losses, many houses remain, and, as listed buildings of historical and architectural interest, they appear to have an assured future. Today, demolition has ceased to be a realistic or legal option, and the historic house has become recognised as worthy of retention and preservation. Public sentiment and interest in the country house has grown, and those that are open to the public receive ever-increasing visitor numbers.

And for those Kent country houses we have lost, they have left their mark with us. In some cases parts of the house survive, and for others foundations and garden features still grace the landscape. Elegant stable blocks and coach houses, often with symmetrical elevations and clock turrets, usually survived the demolition of the house and were converted into attractive residences. This was also the case with estate cottages and lodge houses. We also have postcards, prints, and photographs, as seen in this book, which I hope will serve as a suitable memorial to the country houses of Kent that once were.

Martin Easdown,
August 2017

SECTION 1
EIGHTEENTH CENTURY

The ruins of the grand mansion of Wricklemarsh, Blackheath, in around 1780.

Shurland Hall, Eastchurch – Partially Demolished by the Eighteenth Century

Shurland Hall was erected in the 1520s by Sir Thomas Cheyney to replace the earlier Shurland Castle, constructed by the de Shurland family during the thirteenth century. Sir Thomas, who was Henry VIII's Treasurer of the King's Household, entertained the king there in October 1532 but following his death in 1558, his son Henry abandoned Shurland. Elizabeth I ordered the demolition of much of the house, although what remained was used to house troops. The gatehouse was converted into a farmhouse but this was later abandoned and what survived of the hall steadily became ruinous; however, in recent times, work has been carried out to restore the gatehouse.

Bloor's Place, Rainham – Largely Demolished by the Eighteenth Century

Bloor's Place was a large mansion, erected in the late fifteenth century by Christopher Bloor. However, much of the house was soon destroyed by fire and a further reduction in its size was carried out in the sixteenth and seventeenth centuries, leading to its conversion into a farmhouse. The surviving house is Grade II listed.

Bridge Place, once described as a 'spacious and magnificent mansion', is now just a fraction of the size it once was. The house was erected in 1638 by Sir Arnold Bream, but the cost so impoverished the estate that his heirs were obliged to sell it. In 1704, the house was acquired by John Taylor of nearby Bifrons, who demolished it, save for one wing, which is now Bridge Place Manor and Country Club.

Bridge Place, Bridge – Largely Demolished in 1705

Well Hall, Eltham – Demolished in 1733

Well Hall was a Tudor mansion erected by the eminent Roper family and was set on an island surrounded by a moat. Sir William Roper, Sheriff of Kent in 1553–54, married Margaret, daughter of Sir Thomas More. Well Hall featured a huge painting of More but it was removed when the house was demolished by Sir Gregory Page of Wricklemarsh, who built a new smaller house outside of the moat, which lasted until 1930. The photo shows the surviving Tudor barn, now used as a hire venue for weddings.

Boughton Hall (later Boughton Place) was once home to the influential Wootton family, who were at the courts of Elizabeth I and James I. They enlarged the fourteenth-century manor house during the 1600s, but it later fell into decay and was largely demolished around 1750. The surviving wing is Grade I listed and features Elizabethan plaster ceilings and a stone doorway.

Boughton Hall/Place, Boughton Malherbe – Partially Demolished *c.* 1750

Bore Place, Chiddingstone – Largely Demolished c. 1759

Bore Place was a Tudor mansion that was greatly enlarged by Robert Rede (Lord Chief Justice of the Common Pleas from 1507), and subsequently by Thomas Willoughby during the reign of Henry VIII (1509–47). In 1759, Bore was acquired, and mostly demolished, by Henry Streatfeild from nearby Chiddingstone Castle. What remained became a farmhouse, which is Grade II listed.

Sayes Court (below) dated back to the fifteenth century and was rebuilt during the Elizabethan period. Among its owners was the famous diarist John Evelyn (1620–1706), and in 1698 the house was rented by Peter the Great, Czar of Russia. By 1729 Sayes was in use as a workhouse and remained so until its demolition in 1759.

Sayes Court, Deptford – Demolished in 1759

Brockhull (Thorne), Saltwood – Demolished c. 1760

Brockhull was named after Sir Thomas Brockhull, who was a sheriff and knight of the shire during the reign of Edward III (1327–77). In 1608, the manor was divided by the Tournay family and a new mansion was built in 1611, which survives as part of the Brockhill Performing Arts School. The original mansion was alienated to the Drake-Brockmans, who pulled it down and used the materials to build a bailiff's house (as seen above) near their Beachborough mansion.

The Roper Gate in St Dunstan's Street, Canterbury (below) is the only survivor of the long-lost Tudor Place House, which was home to William Roper and his wife Margaret, daughter of Sir Thomas More. It was pulled down by Sir Edward Hales, who built a new mansion elsewhere on the estate, known as Hales Place (*see* page 34).

Place House, Canterbury – Demolished in 1768

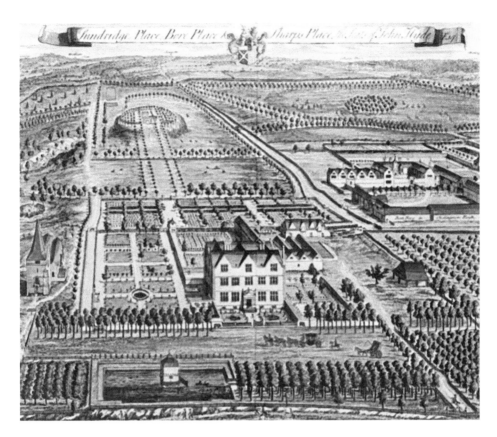

Sundridge Place, Sundridge – Largely Demolished in 1773

Sundridge was an ancient mansion that was owned by the Isley family from the fifteenth century before it was acquired by the Hyde family in the early seventeenth century. They greatly rebuilt the house in the time of Charles I (1625–49), but in 1773 it was largely demolished by John Hyde. The remaining wing was converted into a farmhouse, which is Grade II listed and incorporates a Tudor chimney stack and fireplace.

Wricklemarsh was a Palladian mansion built for Sir Gregory Pope in 1723. It stood in a 250-acre park and was described as 'one of the finest houses in England, resembling a royal palace'. Nevertheless, it became empty and was acquired in 1783 for demolition by John Cater, who was transforming Blackheath into an opulent suburban town. In 1798, only the bare walls of the house remained.

Wricklemarsh, Blackheath – Demolished Between 1783 and 1800

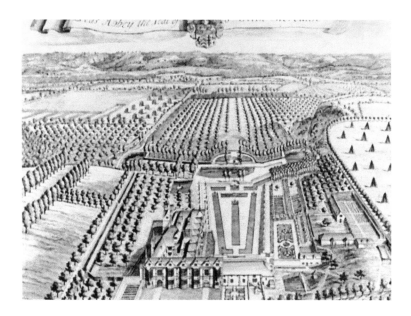

Leeds Abbey House, Leeds – Demolished in 1790
There is very little evidence of either Leeds Abbey/Priory, founded for the Augustinian order in 1119, or the early seventeenth-century house built by the Meredith family on the site. By 1742 the estate stretched to 750 acres, of which 30 acres were formal gardens, but the house quickly fell into disrepair and was demolished in 1790. The estate was used for agricultural use, but hidden away in a wood are the remains of two dovecotes.

Tutsham Hall, once the home of Edward Gulston MP, had become ruinous by the end of the eighteenth century when it was forsaken in favour of nearby Teston Place. The ruins were incorporated into a farmhouse (known as Tutsham Hall), which is Grade II listed.

Tutsham Hall, West Farleigh – Demolished c. 1790

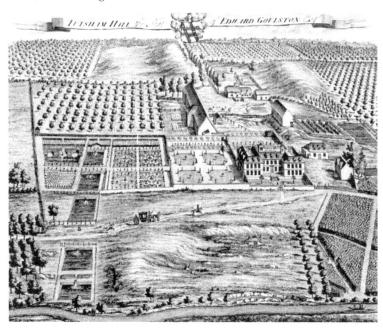

SECTION 2

NINETEENTH CENTURY

Lewisham House, once a grand Tudor mansion – demolished in 1893.

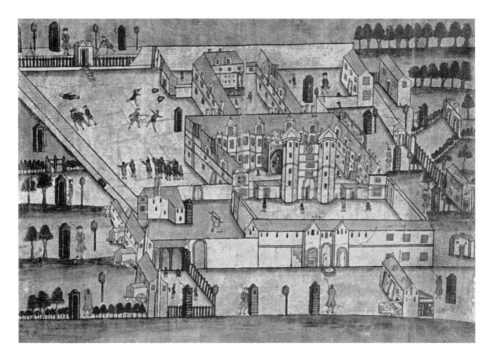

Sissinghurst Castle, Sissinghurst – Largely Demolished by *c.* 1800

Sissinghurst is now an iconic National Trust property, visited by many to see the famous gardens created by Vita Sackville-West and her husband Harold Nicolson, and also its surviving Tudor tower and other buildings. Sissinghurst was not a castle as such, but a large Tudor and Elizabethan mansion created by the Baker family. The finances of the Bakers were ruined during the Civil War and the estate became neglected. In 1756, the mansion was used to house French prisoners of war, who largely wrecked it, and most of the courtyard buildings had been demolished by the end of the eighteenth century. What remained – the tower and its adjoining range, along with the Priest's House and South Cottage – were used as a workhouse and farm before the Nicolsons acquired Sissinghurst in 1930 and began its magical transformation.

South View of QUEKES, at BIRCHINGTON, THANET

Quekes, Birchington – Largely Demolished in 1806

Quekes was built in the fifteenth century by John Queke and from the early sixteenth century it was held by the Crispe family, who held it for 150 years. In 1777, the house was acquired by John Powell-Powell in a ruinous condition. He demolished most of it in 1806, salvaging just a small part that was fashioned into a neoclassical villa. This is still owned by the Powell-Cotton family as part of the Quex Park estate, which features a museum of stuffed animals.

Boxley Abbey House was erected in the Tudor period by the Wyatt family among the remains of a twelfth-century abbey. Alterations were carried out the during the eighteenth century, but in 1815 Lord Aylesford pulled down sixteen bays of the house and fashioned a much smaller property, which still features a fine sixteenth-century rag-stone chimney.

Boxley Abbey House, Boxley – Partially Demolished in 1815

SECOND SCOT'S HALL,
AS REBUILT CIRCA A.D. 1491, FROM AN OLD DRAWING IN THE POSSESSION OF MRS. THOMAS FAIRFAX BEST.

Scot's Hall, Smeeth – Demolition Completed by 1808

Scot's Hall was named after the Scot (or Scott) family, whose first house was situated close to Brabourne Church. In around 1420 they decided to erect a new house further east at Smeeth, which was rebuilt in 1491. A fire subsequently damaged the house and it was rebuilt and enlarged with a grand Elizabethan frontage in around 1634. The fortunes of the family declined during the eighteenth century and in 1784 their Smeeth and Brabourne estates were sold off. Scot's Hall became ruinous, and in 1808 its demolition was completed. In 1798, Hasted records: 'one half part of the mansion of Scott's Hall, with the chapel, was pulled down by Sir John Honywood a few years ago. The remainder is in a very ruinous state.'

THIRD SCOT'S HALL,
AS REBUILT, NEW FRONT, CIRCA A.D. 1634, FROM A DRAWING IN POSSESSION OF CAPT. HENRY SCOTT, R.N.

Lynsted Park, Lynsted – Partially Demolished in 1829

Lynsted Park was built in around 1599 by Sir John Roper to replace an earlier house known as Bedmangore. The house was extended during the seventeenth century but two wings were demolished in 1829 by the incumbent owner, who feared his brother would inherit the house. The surviving portion of the Elizabethan house is Grade II* listed.

Deane (or Dene) Park was the seat of the Oxenden family and was erected during the reign of Elizabeth I (1558–1603). It was described as 'a venerable mansion, large and noble in its appearance'. Following the death of Sir George Oxenden in 1775, the family moved to Broome Park and Deane was subsequently demolished. The Steward's House (Grade II), barns, and part of the stable block can still be seen.

Deane Park, Wingham – Demolished c. 1830

Sevenoaks Park (Park Place), Sevenoaks – Demolished in 1837

Sevenoaks Park (otherwise known as Park Place) was a Palladian-style house erected adjoining Sevenoaks Park in 1654–55 by Thomas Lambarde of Squerries Court, Westerham. The house returned to its original name of Park Place in 1789 when it was improved by Multon Lambard (he did not use the 'e'). In 1837, the house was sold for £15,000 to Colonel Thomas Austen, who promptly demolished it.

Repton Manor dated back to the fifteenth century when it was built by Sir John Fogge, although it was greatly altered in subsequent years. Most of the building, including the south wing, was demolished in the mid-nineteenth century. The surviving brick range, dating from the late sixteenth century and Grade II listed, was used by the military but is now surrounded by new development.

Repton Manor, Ashford – Partially Demolished *c*. 1850

Penge Place, Penge – Demolished in 1853

Penge Place was set in 280-acre grounds, where the boundaries of Kent, Surrey, and London once met. It was rebuilt in a Tudor style by Edward Blore early in the nineteenth century. It was latterly owned by Leo Schuster, a director of the London & Brighton Railway, who happily sold off the house and land for £50,000 to enable the Crystal Palace to be rebuilt on the site. The Jacobean-style lodge to the house in Crystal Palace Park Road can still be seen.

Vine Court was another house built for the powerful Lambarde family in the Sevenoaks area. It was designed by Sir John Vanburgh in around 1720 and was set in 18 acres of land. In 1876 the estate was sold to Charles Hale, who demolished the house to build properties for the 'professional classes'.

Vine Court, Sevenoaks – Demolished in 1876

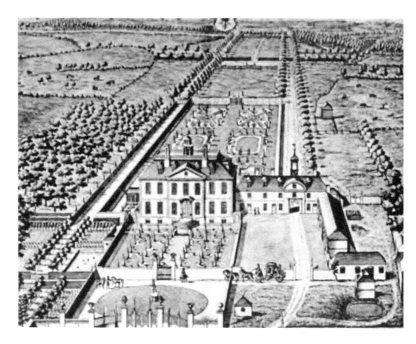

Mount Morris, Monks Horton – Demolished in the Mid-Nineteenth Century

Mount Morris was a handsome seven-bay house erected in around 1695 for the merchant Thomas Morris. The photograph above shows it in 1719 not long after it was built and before it was extended. The park in which it was set was 1,000 acres in extent and featured 300 acres of pasture. It was owned for a time by the eccentric Lord Rokeby, and upon his death in 1800, 13,000 guineas were found in the house because he did not trust banks. Mount Morris was replaced in 1863-64 by the far less grand Monks Horton Manor (below) – otherwise known as Horton Park. This survived until 1999 when it was demolished to make way for a new steel-framed house, infilled with either oak-framed panels or glass. It was completed in 2000.

Monks Horton Manor – Demolished in 1999

Dent-de-Lion, Garlinge – Demolished in the nineteenth century

John Dent de Lion (otherwise known as Daundelyon, or Dandelion) fortified his manor house in 1440. Following his death, five years later, it passed through the Petit family to Henry Fox, Lord Holland, who erected the sham castle and other follies at Kingsgate, near Broadstairs. During the eighteenth century, Dent-de-Lion was rebuilt as a country house and hotel, and the estate was laid out as the Dandelion pleasure grounds, which were popular with visitors from nearby Margate. Following the decline of the attraction, the house was demolished, but the fine fifteenth-century gatehouse survives, complete with the shield of arms of the Dent-de-Lion family. The gatehouse is Grade II* listed.

Dent-de-Lion Gateway, Garlinge, I.o Thanet.

Ellington House, Ramsgate – Demolished in 1892

Dating back to 1270, when it was owned by Nicholas de Elinton, the house gained notoriety in 1652 as its then owner, Adam Sprackling, killed his wife in the house along with six dogs. Sprackling, known for his violent temper when drunk – which he frequently was – tried to escape via tunnels built under the house but was caught trying to set off some gunpowder. In 1866, Edward Hales Wilkie acquired the Ellington estate and sold off most of it for building. The house and remaining surrounding parkland were bought by Ramsgate Corporation in 1892, who demolished the house and opened Ellington Park to the public in 1893. A terrace flint wall in the park was built from remains of the house; it had two foundation stones with the dates '1647' and '1649', but these have been removed for safekeeping.

Section 3

EARLY TWENTIETH CENTURY

The surviving chapel of the long-lost Hales Place in Canterbury, which was demolished in 1928.

Great Bayhall, Pembury – Demolished in 1908

The first mansion at Great Bayhall was built by the famous Kentish Culpepper family in the eleventh century. It passed through some illustrious owners – Humphrey Stafford (Duke of Buckingham), Sir Anthony Browne (Master of the House and Privy Councillor to Henry VIII), and Robert Sackville (Earl of Dorset) – before its acquisition by the Amherst family, who built a grand new house featuring giant pilasters. Anne West was another owner, but following her death in 1803 Bayhall was divided up into cottages. Unfortunately, the cottages were reputed to be haunted so they were abandoned and left to become ruinous, with moss-covered roofs, broken doors and windows, and a clogged-up old moat. The mansion was pulled down in 1908, although some remains survived until 1960. A red-brick barn belonging to the house still survives.

Langley Park, Beckenham – Destroyed by Fire in 1913

Langley Park was named after the Langley family, who acquired the estate in 1350; however, in 1452, Ralph Langley had to sell it to discharge his debts. The estate was subsequently owned by the Stile, Elwill, Raymond, and Burrell families, and in 1838 it was held by E. Goodheart Esq., a magistrate for the county of Kent. In 1884, J. Bucknail acquired the house and 105 acres of land and decided to erect a new residence on the site of the estate's farmhouse. This was built in 1886 and called Langley Court (below). Much of the estate was subsequently sold off for housing development, which commenced in 1909. The old house was converted into a clubhouse for the Langley Park Golf Club in 1910, but was destroyed by fire three years later.

Birling Manor, Birling – Destroyed by Fire in 1917

The 1,800-acre Birling estate has been held by the Nevill family since 1435, when Elizabeth, daughter of Richard Beauchamp, Earl of Worcester, married Sir Edward Nevill. Hasted recorded in 1798 that the old Nevill seat of Birling Place was in use as a farmhouse and an old stone gateway was still in situ. In 1838 William Nevill erected a new house, but this was destroyed by fire on 17 January 1917 when occupied by the widow and family of the late Ralph Nevill (d. 1914). They managed to flee the burning house without sustaining physical harm. The ruins remained in place until after the Second World War but little trace remains now.

Tovil Court, Tovil, Maidstone – Demolished in 1919

Tovil Court stood on a 16-acre estate close to the River Medway and, in the mid-1850s, a widow named Charlotte McKinnon moved in with her three young children using money left for her by her late husband, who had served in the Crimean War. Following Charlotte's death in 1902, the house passed to her surviving children, Lionel and Ada, but following Ada's death in 1905 Lionel decided he had little use for it. The estate was rented out, and for six months in 1914 was home to the Maidstone Zoological and Pleasure Grounds. After Lionel was killed in action in November 1915, Tovil Court passed to Albert Reed, who had founded the nearby Tovil Mills in 1894. He demolished the house to build a working men's club for his workers, and the grounds came to house the Tovil Bowls Club and the Maidstone Masonic Centre.

Greatness, Sevenoaks – Demolished in 1919

Greatness House and its 50 acres of beautiful parkland were laid out in 1763 by a French Huguenot named Peter Novaille III following his marriage to Elizabeth Delamare of Greatness. The estate eventually passed to railway engineer Thomas Crampton in the 1860s, but following his death in 1888 the estate was split up and sold for development. The house became a boys' school called Lansbury College before it was blown up in 1919.

Nackington House dated from the reign of Charles I (1625–49) and was visited by Jane Austen in 1796. By the 1880s the estate comprised of farms, woodland, and 18 acres of gardens, developed by Margaret Waterfield, who resided there until 1914. The house was left ruinous after troops occupied it during the First World War and was demolished in 1921.

Nackington House, Canterbury – Demolished in 1921

Keppleston Ladies School, Beckenham.

Kelsey Park, Beckenham – Demolished in 1921

The original house at Kelsey dated back to 1408, when it was erected by William Kelsiulle. It had been demolished by 1820 and a new house was erected on a different site in a Scottish Baronial style by Richard Bennett, which was enlarged and improved by the Hoare family, who held the estate from 1835–1909. In 1895 the house became a convent, and in 1901 Kepplestone School. The school moved away when 21 acres of the estate was purchased by Beckenham Council in 1909 for £8,800 to create Kelsey Park, which opened in 1913. Other sections of the estate were sold off for housing. The house was used as a military hospital during the First World War, but was left in a poor state at the war's end and it was demolished in 1921.

MILITARY QUARTERS, KELSEY PARK, BECKENHAM. W. J. STEEL, BECKENHAM.

Camp, Gore Court Park, Sittingbourne.

Gore Court, Tunstall, Sittingbourne – Demolished in 1926

Gore Court was built for Colonel Gabriel Harper by S. P. Cockerill in 1792–95 and featured a handsome portico of six Ionic columns. During George Smeed's ownership, between 1853 and 1881, the grounds became well known for its large fêtes, sports events, and band concerts, which continued to be held until 1913. Following Smeed's death, the house was leased out as a school, which was closed at the commencement of the First World War when it was requisitioned as a training camp for soldiers. They left the house in a bad way, and, after failing to be sold at auction, it was demolished in 1926. The bases of two of the Ionic columns can still be seen in King George's Playing Field, and the red-brick Georgian coach house and stables are used as a clubhouse and function hall.

Culverden, Tunbridge Wells – Demolished in 1926

Culverden was an attractive house designed by Decimus Burton, between 1829 and 1830, who also developed nearby Calverley Park. The pleasure grounds were said to have been laid out with much taste and featured an elegant shrubbery and two garden follies – a tower and Swiss Cottage. In 1890, Culverden was acquired by Julius Drew – who founded the Home and Colonial Stores – but was demolished in 1926. The Kent and Sussex Hospital, which opened in 1934, now stands on the site.

Brandfold was a Tudor-style red-brick mansion that was rebuilt in 1872 from an earlier house and remodelled again, by Sir Reginald Blomfield, in 1891 with an Arts and Crafts interior. The house became empty during the First World War and demolition commenced in 1927. The stables and coach house survive as Little Brandfold.

Brandfold, Goudhurst – Demolished in 1927

Hales Place, Canterbury – Demolished in 1928

Hales Place was built by Sir Edward Hales in the late 1760s to replace the Tudor Place House (*see* page 12), which he had pulled down save for the Roper Gate. A Catholic chapel was built on the estate and in 1864 work began to build a Carmelite nunnery to a design by Edward Welby Pugin. However, the money ran out and the building was left unfinished. In the 1880s, Mary Hales was declared bankrupt and the estate passed to a group of exiled French Jesuits, who opened a Catholic boys' school in 1900 called St Mary's College. The estate was put up for sale in 1925 but attracted no buyers, and in 1928 the house was demolished. The grounds were covered with housing, although an early Victorian mortuary chapel (*see* page 25) and one of the gate pillars can still be seen.

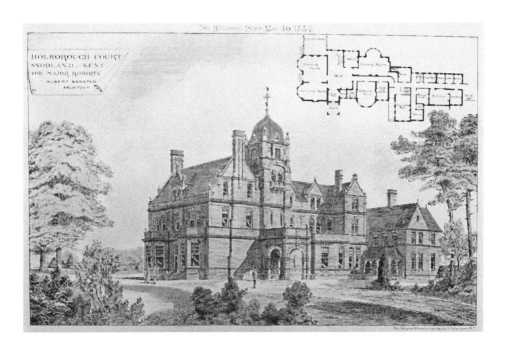

Holborough Court, Snodland – Demolished in 1930

Holborough Court was erected in 1884–86 for William Henry Roberts (1848–1926), who was a partner in the local lime and cement industry. The architect, Hubert Bensted, reused materials from an earlier house called Holloway Court. William Lee Henry Roberts (1871–1928) succeeded his father in both business and owning the house, and upon his death it passed to his nephew, John Cook of Royden Hall, on the condition he took the name Roberts. He did, but promptly sold Holborough Court to Associated Portland Cement Manufacturers (now Blue Circle), who removed it to make way for industrial development. Some of the house's fittings were saved and placed in Paddlesworth Church.

35

Wickham Hall, West Wickham – Demolished in 1931

Wickham Hall dated back to the eighteenth century when Sir Thomas Wilson, High Sheriff of Kent, acquired the Carpenters Farm estate. The house was attached for a time to the Burrell estate at Kelsey, but following its break-up in 1820 Wickham Hall passed through various owners, including the Chairman of the London, Chatham & Dover Railway, Sir James Staat Forbes. In 1883 Gustav Mellin, who had made his fortune inventing baby food, bought the house and during the period 1894–97 he spent £80,000 on doubling its size – at the time it was claimed to be as large as Buckingham Palace. Mellin had only five years to enjoy his grand house before he died, but his wife continued to live there until her death in 1929. Wickham Hall was then demolished, save for the stable block, which was used to house a dairy, printers, and shops before its façade was later incorporated into a Marks and Spencer store.

Chipstead Place, Chevening – Demolished in 1932

Chipstead was derived from the de Chepsted family, who held the manor during the thirteenth century. A new house was erected in the Palladian style by William Emerton around the turn of the eighteenth century. Upon his acquisition of the estate in 1729, Frederick Perkins built an estate village in uniform style by acquiring neighbouring land. However, following his death in 1860, his family had no interest in the house and it was tenanted out, including to railway builder Sir Morton Peto, and banker Henry Oppenheim. During the First World War, the house was used as a military hospital and the estate land began to be sold off. The mansion was last occupied in 1930 before it was stripped of internal fittings and largely demolished, although the ballroom, servants' quarters, and West Lodge survived.

Hayes Place, Hayes – Demolished in 1933

Hayes Place was the home of the distinguished statesman William Pitt, 1st Earl of Chatham, who was prime minister in 1766–68. His son, William Pitt the Younger (the youngest ever prime minister), was born there on 28 May 1759. Pitt acquired Hayes in 1757 then rebuilt the house and added land to the estate. General Wolfe dined there in 1759 on the night before he departed to his fate at Quebec. During Pitt's time as prime minister, Thomas Walpole held the house and encased it in white brick during further enlargement. Walpole resold it to Pitt in 1768, who died there ten years later on 11 May 1778. Other noted owners of Hayes Place include noted philanthropist Edward Wilson (who acquired the house in 1864) and Sir Edward Hambro (1880), who carried out improvements to Hayes village. Hayes Place was demolished in 1933 and houses were erected on the estate.

Blendon Hall, Bexley.

Published by E. Winter, Bexley

Blendon Hall, Bexley – Demolished in 1934

Blendon Hall was once known as Bladindon Court and named after Jordan de Bladindon, who held it during the reign of Richard I (1189–99). A new house was constructed of brick and stucco by Lady Mary Scott in 1765–66 and was castellated with a canted bay on each side of the main entrance. Alterations to the mansion were carried out by banker John Smith in the early years of the nineteenth century, and Humphry Repton was employed to landscape the 90-acre grounds. The last owner of Blendon was Mrs Anna Riggs Jay, and following her death on 28 February 1929 the estate was purchased for development by builder D. C. Bowyer and the house was demolished in 1934. The West Lodge (1855) and some of the trees planted by Repton can still be seen.

Penenden, Penenden Heath – Demolished in 1935

Penenden was erected in around 1830 and was set in 26 acres of grounds containing paddocks, woodland, orchards, a large kitchen garden, and outbuildings – including a gardener's cottage, a double coach house, and stables. It was the home of James Whatman Bosanquet and then his widow Emily until 1899. The house was demolished in 1935 and the grounds developed for housing. The gardener's house survives as Bell Cottage.

Pickhurst Manor had a chequered existence, with owners coming and going and a fire in 1909 that caused £40,000 worth of damage. From the mid-1920s, the estate grounds were laid out for building plots, and during the 1930s the building of houses on the land was accelerated by local builder G. E. Spencer. The house was demolished in 1936.

Pickhurst Manor, Hayes – Demolished in 1936

Trosley Towers, Wrotham – Demolished in 1936

Trosley Towers was an Italianate-styled house built on the crest of a wooded escarpment of the North Downs by Sir Sydney Waterlow in 1887. A bridge, bearing the family crest, was built over the Trottiscliffe Road to connect the two parts of the estate, which can still be seen. Sir Sydney was a politician and philanthropist principally remembered for donating Waterlow Park in north London to the public in 1889 as 'a garden for the gardenless'. Following his death in 1906, the estate passed to his son Philip, who began to sell off some it during the 1920s. After his death in 1931, the remainder of the estate was sold off and the house was demolished in 1936. Trosley Country Park was opened on part of the estate by Kent County Council in 1976.

Bradbourne Hall, Riverhead, Sevenoaks – Demolished in 1937

Bradbourne was noted for having some eccentric owners during its lifetime. One was William Bosville, who, following the death of his wife in 1728, could not bear to live in the house without her and moved into a cottage on the estate. His son Henry also shunned the house. In 1870, Bradbourne acquired another unconventional owner in Francis Crawshay, who placed a bell (the second largest in Kent) in a support next to the house, which could be heard for miles around when it was rung. Crawshay was a druid and erected stone monoliths and a large sundial around the estate. In 1927, the Lambarde family put Bradbourne up for auction and it was acquired by a film company, but in 1937 the house was demolished. Houses were built on the estate but the sundial and some of the monoliths survive in their gardens. The estate lakes can also be seen.

Crete Hall, Northfleet – Demolished in 1938

The original Crete Hall was built by Benjamin Burch (who ran limekilns in the area) in 30 acres of grounds in the 1760s. His son-in-law Jeremiah Rosher (1765–1848) increased the size of the estate to 99 acres and erected a new Crete Hall in 1818. Rosher leased out a disused chalk pit for the creation of the famous Rosherville Gardens – a favoured Victorian pleasure garden for Londoners. His sons George and William – in tandem with architect Henry Edward Kendall – oversaw the creation of a new district called 'Rosherville'. In 1860, the western portion of the estate was sold off to George Sturge and the eastern part became the Harmsworth Printing Works in 1899. The remainder of the estate was acquired by W. T. Henleys, whose works gradually spread to enclose the old Rosherville Gardens. Crete Hall was latterly used by Henleys as a canteen and offices before they demolished it in 1938.

21999 Rosherville Gardens Cafe Chantant.

Evington Place, Elmstead – Demolished in 1938

The distinguished Honywood family owned Evington from the reign of Henry VII (1485–1509) to 1909. Sir John Honywood was High Sheriff of Kent from 1607 to 1609 and his son Edward was created 1st Baronet of Honywood on 19 July 1660. The 2nd Baronet, Sir William Honywood, represented nearby Canterbury, as did the 4th Baronet, Sir John Honywood. In the 1830s, John Edward Honywood built a new house on the site of the old one, but the Honywoods' time at Evington came to end following the death of the 8th Baronet, Sir John William Honywood, on 17 June 1907. The estate was acquired by Lord Ashburton for £24,346 on 24 June 1909; however, on 21 October 1916, he sold it off in individual lots. The house was eventually demolished in 1938.

Montreal, Sevenoaks – Demolished in 1938

Montreal was built by Sir Jeffrey Amherst (1717-97), commander-in-chief of the British forces in the North American campaign of the Seven Years War (1756–63), to replace an earlier house on the site called Brooks Place. He received the surrender of the French at Montreal in 1760 and decided to name his new house in honour of that when construction began in 1764. A large house was constructed in the Palladian style and in 1778 George III stayed there. The Montreal estate grew to encompass 4,000 acres, and revenue was gained from timber and quarrying interests, estate rents, and game shoots. In 1926 the bulk of the estate was sold to Julius Runge, who allowed the house to become ruinous. Following Runge's death in 1936, the estate was sold for development and the house was demolished. An obelisk (commemorating Sir Jeffrey's safe return from North America) and summerhouse survive from the old Montreal estate.

Montreal, Sevenoaks.

Brenley House, Boughton-under-Blean – Demolished in 1938

The first known owner of Brenley was Sir Laurence de Brinley, and during the seventeenth century the house was rebuilt by Sir John Rowth. By the time of the publication in 1838 of *An Epitome of County History Vol. 1: Kent*, the house was held by Edward Jarman and was described as 'a large ancient Elizabethan house, surrounded with agreeable pleasure-grounds'. Brenley subsequently passed into the hands of the Earl Sondes of Lees Court. The house was demolished in 1938 but a two-storeyed range of red-brick stables, dated 1654, and a long brick and timber barn survive. The Hermitage was another house that bit the dust in 1938. It was described as 'a large house, of curious construction, commanding extensive views of the Thames and Medway'. After being used as a hospital in the First World War, it became a monastic school and then a country club, before it was destroyed by fire on 18 August 1938.

The Hermitage, Higham – Destroyed by Fire in 1938

Weardale Manor.

Published by
The Stores, Brasted
W. Withers & Son.

Weardale Manor, Toys Hill, Brasted Chart – Demolished in 1939

Commanding fantastic views of four counties – Kent, East and West Sussex, and Surrey – Weardale Manor was erected in a mock-Tudor style in 1906 by Philip Stanhope, 1st Baron Weardale (1847–1923), a prominent opponent of war and president of the Save the Children Fund. The house had 145 rooms, but was only occupied during the summer months. The gardens were noted for their flowering shrubs (particularly rhododendrons and azaleas) and exotic trees, and for the extensive terracing and lawns on the south side. There was also a kitchen garden and tennis court. Following Philip Stanhope's death, the house was rarely used again (due, it was said, to extensive wet and dry rot, and bad plumbing) and it fell into disrepair before being demolished in 1939. The National Trust now look after the area, where remains of the terracing and a water tower can still be seen.

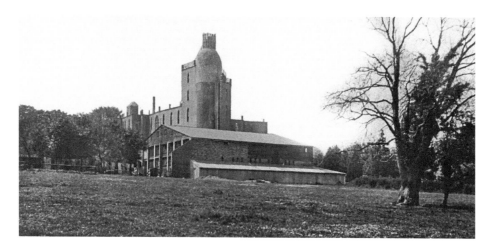

Knockholt House, Knockholt – Demolished in 1942

Both houses were demolished because of enemy action during the Second World War. Knockholt House was an ugly brute of a place with a 120-foot-high tower that housed the chimney flues. It was built in 1890 by James Vavasseur and was soon nicknamed 'Vavasseur's Folly' by locals. Following his death in 1906, there were no takers for the house and while it was lived in by his two unmarried daughters at this time it became increasingly decrepit and the grounds became overgrown. Damage by a landmine led to the house's demolition in April 1942.

Beechmont sat in majestic surroundings overlooking Sevenoaks Weald and was built by the Lambard(e) family in around 1830, who had extensive holdings in the area. Between 1906 and 1920 it was used as a boys' preparatory school, and during the Second World War as an ATS billet. Sadly, in July 1944, the house was hit by a V-1 rocket, killing two women.

Beechmont, Sevenoaks Weald – Demolished in 1944

Fredville House, Nonington – Damaged by Fire and Demolished in 1945

The unusual name, Fredville, comes from the French *'froid de ville'*, meaning 'cold place'. The house was created from a farmhouse in 1750 and was enlarged in 1880 with a large nursery wing to house the Plumptre family. The house, which was visited by Jane Austen in 1811, was noted for its fine parkland with ancient oaks (the 'Majesty Oak' is over a thousand years old) and chestnut trees. In 1918, consideration was given to reducing the size of the house, but instead a new smaller house (named Little Fredville) was erected and the mansion was abandoned. It was later occupied by a girls' school and then by the military in the Second World War. A serious fire in 1945 led to the house being demolished, although the stable block and other outbuildings remain. The attractive thatched-roofed upper and lower lodge houses are Grade II-listed buildings.

The Rookery, Bromley – Destroyed by Fire in 1946

The Rookery was a distinctive house on Bromley Common and home to the Norman family for almost 200 years. Their association with the house began in 1755, and they greatly enlarged it with two wings housing a library and billiard room. Stables and a large greenhouse were erected and a pleasure garden created with a bowling green and a lake. During the Second World War, the house was requisitioned by the military, before suffering a serious fire that led to its demolition in 1946.

Formerly known as Bird's Isle House, The Grange was totally rebuilt in 1897 in Elizabethan style by Joseph Diggle, five times mayor of Tenterden. Between 1915 and 1930 the house was a school, before becoming a rehabilitation centre for jobless men, and then, in 1938, a home for children with learning difficulties. It was damaged by a bomb in September 1940, and the remains were demolished in 1946.

The Grange, St Michaels, Tenterden – Demolished in 1946

Hengherst, Woodchurch – Demolished in the Late 1940s

Originally a fortified residence named after the family that owned it, Hengherst was enlarged by John Charles Schreiber following his inheritance of the estate in 1821. In 1883, Arthur Schreiber added a north wing to the house, which stood in 150 acres of parkland. This featured an avenue of turkey oaks leading to the main road, which were felled during the Second World War to create a landing ground for the military. The house was used as a prisoner-of-war camp and suffered such damage that it had to be demolished. Ileden (below) was another house that suffered damage during the Second World War and had to be demolished – in this instance due to a large fire. The house stood above Barham Downs (close to the present A2) adjoining the Canterbury Racecourse (1729–1879). The farmhouse of the manor of Ileden, largely the eighteenth century, survives and is Grade II listed.

Ileden House, Kingston – Demolished in the Late 1940s after a Fire

Ileden House, Kingstone.

Bifrons, Patrixbourne – Demolished in 1948

Bifrons dates from around 1611 when the first house was completed by John Bargrave, who had prospered as a mercenary soldier and adventurer. An eighteenth-century painting shows the grounds to have extensive walled gardens with an avenue of trees, but they were cleared in around 1750 to make way for formal parkland. Later, in the 1700s, Revd Edward Taylor rebuilt the house (as below) on a new site close by, but in 1807 the Taylors moved out of Bifrons to the nearby Bourne Park and the house was put up for rent. The house was further rebuilt in 1863–64 and let to various tenants; a stable block and coach house were added in 1878. During the Second World War, Bifrons was used as a hostel for free Polish soldiers, but by the war's end it had become very dilapidated and so was demolished in 1948.

SECTION 4

LATE TWENTIETH CENTURY

Hadlow Castle and its lofty tower in 1905.

Addington Place, Addington – Demolished in 1950 after a Fire

The manor of Addington is mentioned in the Domesday Book. By the fifteenth century it was owned by the Watton family, who rebuilt the house in the seventeenth century. In 1886, Addington was acquired by the city banker Joseph Sofer-Whitburn, who engaged Edwin Lutyens to add a south-facing extension, although it did not entirely blend happily with the original house. Sofer-Whitburn died in 1911 and, eventually, in 1933 the house passed to Charles Adams Simpson, who brought his spiritual healing community – the Seekers Trust – to Addington. The mansion was converted into flats and a hotel, and the stable block became small chapels. The Second World War saw the house in use as a rest home for pilots from the nearby West Malling airfield. After the war, the Trust tried to sell Addington, but in 1947 a huge fire engulfed the core of the building. The remainder of the house was demolished in 1950.

Dunsdale, Westerham – Demolished in 1950

The Dunsdale estate was created out of Hill Park Farm, which until the mid-nineteenth century was part of the adjoining Hill Park (later Valence) estate (*see* page 86). In 1854, Joseph Kitchen engaged architect Robert Kerr to design a mansion in the Victorian Gothic Revival style. Upon the house's completion in 1858, Edward Milner was hired to landscape the gardens. In 1880, Kitchen's assets were put into liquidation and handled by trustees until both Dunsdale and Hill Park were acquired by Norman Watney. Dunsdale was tenanted out and during the First World War it was used as a Red Cross hospital. The gardens became neglected, and in 1949 the Dunsdale estate was acquired by developer Llewellyn Jones, who demolished the house. Surviving features include a gate lodge, walled kitchen garden and a lake with a bridge. A new house was erected in 1999.

Foots Cray Place, Foots Cray – Demolished in 1950 after a Fire

This was an elegant and unusual English country house built to the Palladian design of Andrea Palladio's Villa Rotunda (as was the surviving Mereworth Castle). The house was commissioned by Bourchier Cleeve in 1754 and was described as 'a design of Palladio of the Ionic order, and peculiarly elegant. The hall is octagonal, and has a gallery, ornamented with busts leading to the bed-chambers'. The house was acquired by Nicholas Vanisittart in 1821 for £28,000 (who also owned the adjoining North Cray Place), but it was often leased out and in 1898 passed to Samuel Waring, who improved the gardens and estate. He died in 1940 and the house became a naval training establishment, but was left in a poor condition at the war's end. It was acquired by Kent County Council, who planned to open a museum, but sadly the building was badly damaged by fire on 18 October 1949 and subsequently demolished.

Cale Hill, Little Chart – Demolished in 1952

Cale Hill was a distinctive mansion flanked by two side pavilions, one of which remains today. Other surviving relics include the South Lodge and remains of the original 1438 house, which have been incorporated into Calehill House and feature a window of two cinquefoil-headed lights. Cale Hill was named after the hundred (a historical land division) in which it was situated and was owned by the Darell family from 1410 until the twentieth century. In 1753–54, Sir Philip Darell built a new house to the south-east of the original, which was described in *An Epitome of County History* (1838) as 'a fine substantial mansion, situated on a gentle elevation, and surrounded by beautiful and fertile grounds. The interior is very elegant; the furniture, in the drawing room particularly, is superb'. Sadly, after becoming ruinous, Cale Hill was largely demolished in 1952.

Castle Gates Hadlow Kent

Hadlow Castle, Hadlow – Demolished in 1952

Hadlow Castle was a huge Gothic mansion that took over sixty years to build – its lofty tower still dominates the area. Its creator was Walter May, who inherited Hadlow Court Lodge in 1786 and set about transforming it in the most extraordinary way. The chosen architect was the relatively unknown J. Dugdale. The tower was added by May's son, Walter Barton May, and architect George Ledwell Taylor to a height of 170 feet in 1838–40. It was soon nicknamed by locals 'May's Folly'. The interior of the house featured a 120-foot-long corridor running east to west, with a large stained-glass window at each end. Following military occupation during the Second World War, the house was in a bad condition and demolished. Fortunately, the tower was saved (along with the entrance arches, lodges, and stable court) and has been restored.

Hadlow Castle Kent

Halstead Place, Halstead – Demolished in 1952

The origins of Halstead Place were a manor house, which, during the time of Edward IV (1461–83), was owned by Thomas Bourchier, Archbishop of Canterbury. During the 1770s, the house was rebuilt in the surroundings of a beautiful park and was later occupied by Alderman John Atkins (c. 1760–1838), a former mayor of London, MP, and deputy lieutenant of the county of Kent. His daughter Anna Atkins (1799–1871) was a renowned botanist and photographer. In 1927 Halstead was being used as a school, but was requisitioned by the Home Office in the Second World War before becoming a prisoner of war camp. The house was left in a poor condition after the war and was pulled down in 1952; it was replaced by a school, which was subsequently demolished. The coach house, stable block (with a bell dated '1772'), and gatehouse survive from the old house.

Wootton Court, Wootton – Demolished in 1952

The manor of Wootton changed hands frequently until it came into the ownership of John Brydges in 1704. He died in 1712 and his two sons, John and Edward, both resided there until their deaths in 1780. Edward's eldest son, Reverend Edward Tymewell Brydges, inherited Wootton and approached architect John Plaw to rebuild the mansion. The adjoining gardens and parkland were also greatly improved. In the 1860s, the house was sold to George Joseph Murray, who remodelled it with a new brick and flint elevation. It was later used as a school, before being used to hold prisoners of war during the Second World War, who left it in a derelict state. The inevitable demolition followed in 1952. The coach house and stables were converted into two homes in the 1970s.

Beachborough Park, Newington – Partially Destroyed by Fire in 1953

Anciently known as Bilcheborough, Beachborough was acquired by Henry Brockman in around 1600, who carried out an extensive rebuilding of the house. In 1767, it was bequeathed by James Brockman to his cousin Revd Ralph Drake with an injunction that he took the surname and arms of the Brockman family. Sir James Drake-Brockman rebuilt the house in 1813, but in 1897 the Drake-Brockmans left and Beachborough passed to a Board of Trustees, who rented it out. Between 1902 and 1910 the tenant was future Prime Minister David Lloyd George. During the First World War, Beachborough was home to a Canadian military hospital, and then it became a private school – Stowe College – for twenty years. Sadly, fire destroyed the front and central ranges of the house in 1953 during refurbishment, leaving three isolated fragments, including the portico. The clock with the date '1813' was saved and relocated on the surviving western wing of the house.

Surrenden Dering, Pluckley – Damaged by Fire in 1952 and Largely Demolished in 1953
Surrenden Dering was a red-brick mansion that was rebuilt by Sir Edward Dering in the 1630s. It featured Dutch gables and the famous arched Dering windows, which can still be seen on properties in the Pluckley area. In 1763, the house was enlarged by 5th Baronet Edward Dering, and further rebuilding was carried out by William Burn between 1840 and 1857 when the Dering arched windows were added. The house was rented out after 1896, and 1,795 acres of the outlying farmland was sold off in 1918. Ten years later, in 1928, Sir Henry Dering sold off the remaining 3,824 acres and the contents of the house, which was used by Northaw School. However, in 1952, a fire badly damaged the house and it was demolished, save for the north service wing, which is now Surrenden House. Estate buildings and garden features can also still be seen.

Vinters, near Maidstone

Vinters, Maidstone – Badly Damaged by Fire in 1952 and Demolished in 1954

Vinters dated back to 1343, when Roger de Vinter bought land from the abbott of Boxley and built a typical three-room open hall house of the period. The mansion, which was demolished in 1952, was the creation of the Whatman family, who ran the nearby Turkey Court paper mill. James Whatman acquired the estate in 1782; as well as greatly improving the house, he spent around £5,000 on landscaping the estate. Whatman's grandson, also a James, carried out further improvements to the house and grounds in 1852. However, the Whatmans moved out in 1912 and the house was rented out, though it was often empty. Vinters was another country house ruined by military occupation in the Second World War and was demolished following a fire. The grounds were developed with housing, with the exception of 90 acres that form the Vinters Valley Nature Reserve.

East Cliff Lodge, Ramsgate – Demolished in 1954

Noted as the home of the great Jewish Philanthropist Sir Moses Montefiore, the building of East Cliff Lodge was commenced in 1794 and it became the summer residence of Queen Caroline when she was Princess of Wales. Other inhabitants included Admiral Lord George Keith and Marquis Wellesley (brother of the Duke of Wellington) before it was rented by Sir Moses in 1822. He bought the house eight years later for £5,500 and lived there until his death in 1885 at the age of 101. The house and grounds were acquired by Ramsgate Council in 1938, who demolished the house in 1953–54. The grounds were laid out as a public park and feature the Grade II* Italianate greenhouse (pictured) erected by George Keith in 1805. The gatehouse and stable block of the house survive and are Grade II listed.

Hothfield Place, Hothfield – Demolished in 1954

Hothfield was a rather plain mansion, erected in 1778–80 for Sackville Tufton, 8th Earl of Thanet to replace a Tudor house. It was probably designed by Samuel Wyatt and was set in a 1,815-acre estate that was said to be one of the most affluent in the county, with its own gasworks and fire station. However, by the time of the 1st Lord Hothfield's death in November 1926, the estate was struggling and outlying areas were subsequently sold off. The house was damaged by a flying bomb in 1944 while it was in use as a prisoner of war camp. Then, after being sold off in 1947, the house was finally demolished in 1954. A new dwelling, Polla House, was built south of the old mansion, whose kitchen garden, lodge house, farm manager's house, and stable block can still be seen.

LEE PRIORY,
SOUTH WEST VIEW
KENT

Lee Priory, Littlebourne – Demolished in 1954

Lee Priory was a striking Gothic mansion, noted for its distinctive spire, and was built for Thomas Barrett by James Wyatt in 1783–85. By 1838, when John William Egerton Brydges was the estate holder, the house was described as 'a fine specimen of Gothic architecture with a good collection of paintings'. Between 1860 and 1863 the house was altered and extended by George Gilbert Scott, who added a service wing, which survived the demolition of the house. Wyatt's service court also remains and is entered from the north through a castellated, four-centred archway. The surviving eighteenth-century stables feature two big arches under a pediment. The house itself was demolished after the death of Marmaduke Ramsey on 31 December 1947 (who had acquired it in 1919) but the famous vaulted Strawberry Room was rescued and re-erected in the Victoria and Albert Museum in London.

Elvington Court, Eythorne – Demolished in the 1950s

Elvington Court ended up having a rather unusual life for a country house: it became dormitory accommodation for miners working in the Kent Coalfield. Dating back to the first quarter of the eighteenth century, and formerly known as Street End House, Elvington Court was lying empty when it was leased by Arthur Burr in 1906. Burr was head of Kent Coal Concessions Ltd, who were developing collieries in east Kent (with various degrees of success) and a new mining village was provided at Elvington for miners working at nearby Tilmanstone Colliery. The mansion was fitted out with dormitories for miners, who were charged 25s a week for full board. Burr resigned in 1914 after being accused of fraud and his successor, Richard Tilden Smith, converted the barn at Elvington Court into a miner's leisure centre. The house was demolished in the 1950s but three smaller buildings of the estate survive.

Nethercourt House, St Lawrence, Ramsgate – Demolished in 1957

Nethercourt was held by Nicholas de Sandwich during the reign of Edward III (1327–77) and frequently changed hands during the ensuing centuries. By the time of Queen Anne (1702–14), it was held by Edward Brook and rebuilt. Subsequently, the house became a farmhouse and vicarage. It was demolished in 1957 and a housing estate was built in the grounds, although the old gatehouse still stands.

Park House was formerly part of the Boxley Abbey estate (*see* page 17) and was built by Sir Mawdistly Best, a professional soldier, in 1876. Following his death in 1906, both Park House and Boxley Abbey passed to his niece, but in the 1950s – with death duties to pay – the family chose to live at Boxley Abbey and Park House was demolished. The coach house and stable block were converted into houses.

Park House, Boxley – Demolished in 1957

Dunorlan Park, Tunbridge Wells – Demolished in 1958

Dunorlan was a controversial building, once described by a servant who worked there as 'an architectural monstrosity which represented everything one might expect from a man with too much money and too little taste'. That man was Henry Reed, who was not that happy himself with the house when it was built in 1862 and demolished part of it to build a new wing. During the Second World War, Dunorlan came into the hands of the War Damage Commission, who sold it to Tunbridge Wells Council in 1957 for £42,000. They demolished the house and opened the surrounding parkland to the public. Nearby Great Bounds Manor was rebuilt around 1600 and changed hands frequently before it was acquired by the Reliance Mutual Co. in 1939. They moved out in 1958 and the house and grounds were sold for development, although the Grade II-listed lodge house survives – west of the Tonbridge–Southborough road.

Great Bounds Manor, Southborough – Demolished in 1958

Belvedere, Erith – Demolished in 1959

Belvedere was erected in 1741 by Thomas Hayley to take advantage of the magnificent views of the River Thames. In 1762 it passed to Baron Eardley of Spalding, who engaged James Stuart to rebuild the house on a much grander scale. Stuart demolished most of the building, save for the Gold Room, which was constructed to receive George III (1760–1820). The new house featured a portico supported by six Ionic columns, but was otherwise rather undistinguished and it was abandoned by Sir Culling Eardley in the 1850s following the polluting of the river by the Crossness sewage works. Eardley began to develop the grounds as a dormitory suburb called Belvedere, and, following his death in May 1863, the remainder of the estate was sold for housing and the mansion was acquired for £12,148 by the Shipwrecked Mariner's Society as a seaman's home. The house was eventually pulled down in 1959.

Sailors Home   Belvedere

Kearsney Abbey, near Dover.

Kearsney Abbey, Kearsney – Demolished in 1959

Kearsney Abbey was erected in 1822 and despite its name had no ecclesiastical connection, though much of its dressed stonework was acquired from ancient buildings demolished in Dover. In 1884, the Fector family sold the house and it subsequently passed through a bewildering succession of auction sales and owners. During the Second World War, Kearsney was requisitioned by the War Department for use as an ATS establishment, and, upon the resumption of peace, the house and 25 acres of grounds were sold to Dover District Council. They laid out the grounds as a public park and demolished the house due to severe dry rot, save for the billiard room, which is in use as a popular café. In 2014, the Heritage Lottery fund awarded £3.1 million for a major restoration of the Kearsney Abbey grounds, along with the neighbouring Russell Gardens. The café will be extended to become a multipurpose venue.

May Place, Crayford – Demolished in 1959

May Place was built in 1603 for the Appleton family on rising ground above the old manor house. Its most famous owner was Admiral Sir Cloudesley Shovell (1650–1707), who found fame during the War of the Spanish Succession (1702–14) when he helped capture Gibraltar in 1704. Unfortunately, Shovell was to meet a grisly end when he was strangled by a greedy fishwife for his emerald ring after being washed ashore from a stricken vessel on 22 October 1707. In 1903 the house, which had remained empty for many years, was converted into a clubhouse for a golf course laid out in the grounds. However, during the 1930s, the estate began to be developed for housing. The mansion suffered damage during the Second World War, which led to its subsequent demolition by Crayford Council.

Shoreham Place, Shoreham – Destroyed by Fire in 1959

For over a century – from the 1830s to the 1940s – Shoreham Place was home to the Mildmay family, whose name is immortalised in horse racing circles at the Mildmay course at Aintree and the Mildmay of Flete Challenge Cup at the Cheltenham Festival. This was to down to Anthony, 2nd Lord Mildmay, a renowned amateur steeplechaser who kindled Queen Elizabeth the Queen Mother's interest in steeplechasing. The house was built in 1838 close to the site of an Italian-style mansion called the New House, which was demolished a few years earlier because it was too damp to live in. Shoreham Place was built in yellow-stock brick and was described by Helen Mildmay-White as 'ugly but very comfortable', but in 1959 it was destroyed by fire. A new housing estate was built on its site in 1964, although the stable block survives as residential buildings.

Redleaf House, Chiddingstone – Demolished in the 1950s

The old house at Redleaf was demolished in 1883–84 by Frank Hills and a new one in a Gothic Revival style was built. The outlying areas of the estate were sold off during the 1920s to pay for death duties, and the house and stable block were demolished around thirty years later; however, the entrance lodges, head gardener's house, walled garden, and other garden features still survive.

Heppington was an Elizabethan mansion that gained a Queen Anne exterior in 1710 after it was acquired by Brian Faussett. The Faussetts owned Heppington until 1899, after which it passed to the Chapman family, who held it until just after the Second World War. It then passed to Nackington Farms, who housed their workers in the house, and then their chickens, before it was demolished in 1960.

Heppington House, Nackington – Demolished in 1960

Wounded Belgian Soldiers at Holbrook Hospital (Temporary), Chislehurst. 16/10/1914.

Holbrook House, Chislehurst – Demolished in 1960

Holbrook House has been better documented for its wartime use and not much is known about its peacetime life. During the First World War, it was fitted out as a Red Cross hospital and was used to house wounded Belgian soldiers (above). The mansion was commandeered again during the Second World War and this time suffered considerable damage. A small development of apartments, and a residential care home now cover where it once stood.

Falconhurst was designed in a Jacobean style by David Brandon for John Chetwynd-Talbot in 1850–52 and was added to by John Duke Coleridge in 1913. Brandon's work was demolished, however, in 1960–61, due to severe dry rot, with only a few walls surviving, including the main doorway with the family coat of arms carved above it. The Chetwynd-Talbots still own the estate and hire it out for weddings and other functions.

Falconhurst, Markbeech – Partially Demolished in 1961

North Cray Place, the Seat of the Revd William Hetherington, A.M.

North Cray Place, North Cray – Demolished in 1961

North Cray Place stood on the other side of the River Cray from the rather more handsome Foots Cray Place (*see* page 56) and in 1781–82 Thomas Coventry engaged Capability Brown to lay out a park, which included an elegant five-arch bridge over the Cray. A new house was built in 1823 to a design by Henry Walker. By 1833, both North and Foots Cray were owned by Nicholas Vansittart, Lord Bexley. However, during the Vansittart's ownership – up until 1918 – North Cray was often leased out, including, in 1908, to the North Kent Golf Club. The end for the house came after it was hit by a bomb in 1944, although it was not finally cleared away until houses were built on the site. The local authority purchased the parklands of both North Cray and Foots Cray to create the Foots Cray Meadows Parkland.

Syndale Park, Ospringe – Damaged by Fire and Mostly Demolished in 1961

Daniel Judd built a mansion on this site in 1652 after making his fortune in the gunpowder industry on land taken away from the dean and chapter of Rochester. However, on the restoration of the monarchy in 1660, the dean and chapter claimed the land back and Parliamentarian Judd was ejected from the house. In 1838, Syndale, as it was now known, was described in *An Epitome of County History* as 'an elegant structure, built after a design of Inigo Jones: the front is relieved with pilasters, crowned with rich capitals. This mansion stands in the centre of a picturesque park ... and the interior is elegantly fitted-up'. Sadly, in 1961, a fire destroyed much of the house. What remained was incorporated into the Syndale Park Hotel, which has now been renamed Judd's Folly Hotel.

Bickley Hall, Bickley – Demolished in 1963

Bickley Hall dated back to 1780, and was extended in 1812 when John Wells engaged Sir Robert Smirke to carry out alterations. However, Wells was declared bankrupt in 1841 and the outer estate grounds were sold to a developer. The house eventually became a school in 1908 but, following the school's closure, it was demolished to make way for an estate of detached houses.

Southend Hall started life as a seventeenth-century farmhouse, before it was enlarged by the Latter family around 1850 with a gabled extension, a tower topped with a cupola, and an attractive round conservatory. In 1937, the house was sold to the Ministry of Defence to house an air-defence unit; it was later used by the Civil Defence Corps and Territorial Army. In 1969 the decision was taken to sell Southend Hall, and it was demolished two years later to make way for housing.

Southend Hall, Eltham – Demolished in 1971

Norton Court, Norton, near Faversham – Partially Destroyed by fire in 1966

Norton Court was built in 1625 for the Milles family, reputedly by Inigo Jones, but during the seventeenth and eighteenth centuries it changed hands frequently. Probably the most distinguished owner of the house was the Right Hon. Stephen Rumbold Lushington, MP for Canterbury from 1812–30 and 1835–37. In 1910, the building was restored by Sir Reginald Blomfield, but in 1966 the main range was destroyed by fire. The surviving section, which is Grade II listed, was the service wing and dates from the late seventeenth century (below). It features the painted Monk's Room, decorated by a fugitive Catholic recusant when it was first built. Norton Court Lodge and the courtyard are also listed buildings.

Walmer Place, Walmer – Demolished in 1966

This Italianate seaside residence was built in 1902 on the site of a Queen Anne house, and was let to wealthy shipping merchant and banker James Marke Wood. Following his death in 1908, his widow Agnes acquired the house at auction and lived there until she died in 1927. Walmer Place then passed to her daughter, Contessa Di Sant' Elia, who tended to spend more time in the lodge on the estate as it was protected from cold sea winds, or in London. In 1958 the house was put up for sale, but two years later it was damaged by a fire that started in the basement. The Contessa died in January 1965, and in the following year Walmer Place was demolished to make way for blocks of flats. Remains of the garden terrace can still be seen from the road fronting the beach.

24./5. 13.

High Elms, Farnborough – Destroyed by Fire in 1967

High Elms was home to the wealthy banking family, the Lubbocks (1809–1938) one of whom, the 4th Baronet, helped introduce the August bank holiday in 1870. His father, John William Lubbock (1803–65), the 3rd Baronet, was a great friend of Charles Darwin, who lived nearby at Down House. He erected a new mansion in 1842, designed by Philip Hardwick in an Italianate style and set in ornamental gardens. In 1938, the 250-acre estate was sold to Kent County Council and the last member of the Lubbock family left the house in 1947. The London borough of Bromley took over the estate in 1965 and created High Elms Country Park and a golf course. The house was destroyed by fire in 1967 but the stable block, terraced gardens, and garden buildings – such as an Eton Fives Court – can be seen in the country park.

Woodstock, Tunstall, Sittingbourne – Demolished in 1972

Woodstock was erected around 1780 by Abraham Chambers and *An Epitome of County History* (1838) describes it as: 'a fine handsome building, seated on a gentle elevation, in a well wooded park. The interior is spacious and elegant, and ornamented with a small collection of paintings by Sir Peter Lely and others'. In 1919, the Twopenny family sold the house to the wealthy banker John Francis Gilliat (1883–1948), who was married to the Marchioness of Anglesey. They largely abandoned Woodstock in 1930 to live in London and it was tenanted out before being used as a hospital during the Second World War. Part of the estate was subsequently purchased by Shell Oil Co. to build a research complex, but the house, which had become steadily derelict, was demolished by Shell in 1971–72.

WOODSTOCK PARK, SITTINGBOURNE.

SECTION 5

HOUSES RELOCATED, RESTORED, REBUILT

The old and new houses at Scotney, 2017.

Ingress, Greenhithe – Demolished in 1833 and Replaced by a New House

The fine neo-Gothic house known as Ingress Abbey can still be found overlooking the southern bank of the River Thames at Greenhithe, although its estate grounds are largely covered with new housing. The original house was famed for its extensive pleasure gardens and follies, some of which can still be seen. In 1748, Ingress was acquired by William Ponsonby and, over the next decade, a Doric temple, Ionic temple (now at Cobham Hall), Chinese temple, and bridge, grottos and caves were added. Ponsonby's successor, John Calcraft, engaged Capability Brown to landscape the gardens and William Chambers to carry out alterations to the house. It was during the ownership of James Harmer that the present house was built, slightly to the east of its predecessor on the site of a former coach house.

Scotney Castle, Lamberhurst – Partially Demolished in 1837 and Replaced by a New House

The old house at Scotney is famed as the picturesque ruin centrepiece of the National Trust garden, which was bequeathed to them by Christopher Hussey – an authority on country houses – in 1970. Scotney was built as a fortified manor house between 1378 and 1380 by Roger de Ashburnham and featured four corner towers (one of which still survives) and a surrounding moat. By the mid-sixteenth century the castle was ruinous and in 1580 it was rebuilt as a country residence by Thomas Darell, with a new Elizabethan wing. During the 1720s Georgian additions were added to the house, and the surviving tower received a conical roof and cupola. However, in 1837, Edward Hussey took the decision to abandon the house and build a new residence on higher ground, which was designed by Anthony Salvin and completed in 1843. The Georgian wings of the old house were demolished to create the romantic ruin we see today.

HILL PARK,
KENT

Hill Park, Westerham – Demolished in 1886 and Replaced by a New House Called Valence

Valence was the original name of the estate and is attributed to Haimo de Valoines, who acquired the deeds in 1147–48 to ten parcels of land. In 1717, Peter Manning built a large dwelling house. Upon its acquisition by the Earl of Hillsborough in 1771, he changed the name to Hill Park and rebuilt it. Capability Brown was hired to landscape the grounds and add a lake (at a cost of £1,200), and a model dairy, resembling a grand rotunda, was added. In 1836, Hill Park was acquired by David Baillie for £16,000 and he remodelled the house with a conservatory and formal parterres to the north and south. However, in 1886, new owner Norman Watney demolished Hill Park to build a new mansion to the south-west (below), restoring the old name of Valence. Today, the building is being used as a school.

Great Maytham Hall, Rolvenden – Badly Damaged by Fire in 1893 then Demolished and Rebuilt in 1909

The original house was built by Captain James Monypenny in 1721, although it remained uncompleted and roofless until 1760 when it was finished by his son James. In 1880, the house was rebuilt in a mock-Tudor style by Colonel Robert Gibbon-Monypenny but suffered a serious fire in 1893. However, it was patched-up and leased out to various tenants, including author Frances Hodgson Burnett between 1898 and 1907. She used the neglected walled garden as the inspiration for her famous Children's book *The Secret Garden* (1911). Between 1909 and 1912 a new house was erected by Sir Edwin Lutyens for H. J. Tennant (a Liberal MP), utilising the core and basement of the old house. The building was designed in the style of Christopher Wren and cost £24,000. The grounds were landscaped by Lutyens' cohort Gertrude Jekyll. The house is now fifteen flats and Grade II listed.

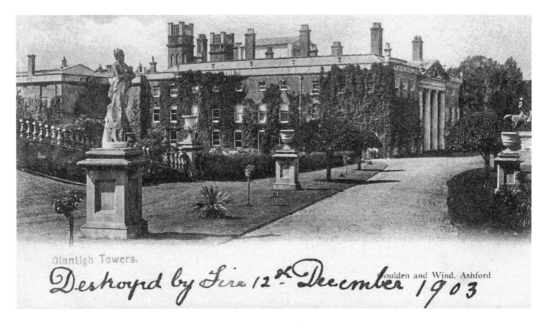

Olantigh Towers.

Destroyed by Fire 12ᵗʰ December 1903

oulden and Wind. Ashford

Olantigh Towers, Wye – Destroyed by Fire in 1903 and Rebuilt in 1912

In 1508, Thomas Kempe gave his new house the name Olantigh, which means 'holly enclosure'. In 1768, John Sawbridge rebuilt and extended the house and added a massive stone portico, which was the only survivor of the December 1903 fire that destroyed the building. In 1851 John Samuel Wanley Sawbridge Erle-Drax, known as the Mad Major, inherited Olantigh. He added two Venetian towers and two huge picture galleries, and commissioned a statue of himself and his favourite charger, which can still be seen hidden away in woodland on the estate. Following the 1903 fire, the house was rebuilt to a smaller size, incorporating the portico, and following completion in 1912, it was let to J. H. Loudon, whose son F. W. H. Loudon acquired it in 1935. In the mid-1950s, the west wing was demolished. The stables of the old house are Grade II listed.

Lees Court, Sheldwich – Destroyed by Fire in 1910 and Rebuilt in 1912

Lees Court acquired its name from the Atte-Leese family, who owned the estate during the reign of Edward I (1272–1307). In 1652, Sir George Sondes rebuilt the mansion, possibly to a design by Inigo Jones. It featured an impressive frontage with an unbroken stucco façade of thirteen bays, adorned with fourteen Ionic pillars and surmounted by an overhanging roof. Sadly, during the morning of Sunday 21 November 1910, the mansion was destroyed in a huge fire. Around £200,000 worth of damage was caused, although paintings, furniture, glass, silver, and the vault containing the Sondes family treasures, was rescued. The house was quickly rebuilt in the same style. Upon the death of the 4th Earl Sondes in 1970, Lees Court was acquired for conversion into luxury apartments. It is now a Grade I listed building and surviving remnants from the original house include the lodge and stables, which were built in 1786.

Oxney Court, Ringwould – Destroyed by Fire in the First World War and Rebuilt from 1997
This is a house that literally came back from the dead, having been ruinous and deserted for nearly eighty years before it was restored to its Edwardian splendour. The parish of Oxney is one of the smallest in Kent, and during the Tudor period Oxney Court was enlarged by John Smedley, a senior officer at the treasury. The late seventeenth century saw the timber-framed house rebuilt in red brick; over the next fifty years it was restyled with a Gothic look and extended with a drawing room wing, tower, and entrance porch. In around 1838 Edward Banks acquired Oxney, with his family holding it just a year short of 100. However, during army occupation in the First World War, the house was left a charred ruin. Stories grew over the years of mysterious goings-on at the house, along with ghostly sightings on the nearby Dover–Deal road, but after Oxney's restoration the spirits now can rest in peace.

Eastwell House, near Ashford

Eastwell Park, Boughton Aluph and Eastwell – Demolished in 1926 and Replaced by a New House

Eastwell is one of the largest enclosed parks in Kent (1,200 acres in 1838) and at its heart is what looks like an Elizabethan mansion, serving as a country house hotel and restaurant called Eastwell Manor. However, the house actually only dates from the 1920s, when it replaced a genuine sixteenth-century mansion. It was subsequently rebuilt in 1793–99, and again in 1849. From 1874–93 Eastwell was rented by Prince Alfred, second son of Queen Victoria, who was a frequent visitor. The prince's daughter, Princess Marie, was born at Eastwell in 1875 and wrote of 'beautiful Eastwell, with its great grey house, its magnificent park, with its herd of deer and picturesque Highland cattle, its lake, its woods, its garden with the old cedar tree, which was our fairy mansion'. A gatehouse built in 1848 – of a striking design – stands around a mile to the south of the house.

Great Swifts Manor, Cranbrook – Demolished in 1936 and Replaced by a New House
Stephen Swift gave his name to the house during the fifteenth century. By 1664, it was owned by the Cooke family, who enlarged and renamed it Great Swifts. Under the ownership of cricket lover Robert Tooth, Great Swifts hosted a Kent vs England match in 1851 and two Kent county games in the early 1860s. Lieutenant-Colonel Boyd Alexander was the next owner – his son Boyd is credited with discovering Lake Chad in Africa. Following his son's death in 1910 at the hands of natives, the colonel produced a replica of the lake in the grounds of Great Swifts. In 1936, Peter Cazalet MP acquired the estate and built a new house, which was completed two years later. Among the visitors to Cazalet's new house was his goddaughter Elizabeth Taylor. In 2012 the estate was sold for £9 million, having been renamed Oak Hill Manor estate.

Sandling Park, Saltwood – Damaged by Enemy Action in 1942 and Replaced by a New House
Sandling Park is described in *An Epitome of County History* (1838) as 'a modern structure, built towards the end of the last century (1796) by William Deedes, Esq, under the direction of Joseph Bonomi, the architect. It stands on an elevation in the park, at the distance of a mile from the lodge entrance, on the Hythe and Ashford road. The park is well wooded, and exhibits great diversity of scenery. The house has a stately appearance, and is sheltered from the north-west by plantations and shrubberies'. In 1897 the estate passed to the Hardy family, who still own it, and they built the present house in 1949 to a design by E. D. Jefferiss Matthews. The gardens are famous for their azaleas and rhododendrons and when they are in bloom in May the garden is open to the public for charitable purposes.

Capel Manor, Horsmonden – Demolished by 1969 and Replaced by a New House

Capel Manor was an Italianate mansion built by John Francis Austen between 1859 and 1862 – a descendant of novelist Jane Austen, who visited various Kent country houses. The architect T. H. Wyatt built the house of cream, green, and brown sandstone for a polychromatic effect. The house was used by the army during the Second World War and was left damaged and unoccupied. By 1969, the remains of the building were removed to enable a new house to be built by architect Michael Manser for John Howard, private personal secretary to Prime Minister Edward Heath. Manser's modern labour-saving house, completed in 1970 and designed as a simple single-storey glass and steel structure, has become revered as a modernist icon and is Grade II listed. The arcaded frontage of the retaining wall, along with a grand flight of steps, were retained from the old house. Other remaining features include the two lodge houses.

Harbourne Hall, High Halden – Demolished in 1980

These two mansions were demolished in the 1980s to make way for new houses. Harbourne Hall was a red-brick Italianate house, built for Henry Latter by C. G. Wray in 1875 and noted for its distinctive tower. It was erected on the site of an earlier house that had associations with the Ransleys – a notorious smuggling family. South Park only underwent a partial demolition as a section of the house, including the Gothic tower and terracing, were incorporated into the new building. These are Grade II listed. The original house was completed in 1773 and became the seat of Henry Hardinge (1785–1856), 1st Viscount of Lahore and Governor-General of India. In 1844, the house was enlarged by Anthony Salvin and extended again during the twentieth century, although these additions were demolished in 1989.

South Park, Penshurst – Partially Demolished in 1989

95

SOURCES AND ACKNOWLEDGEMENTS

The postcards and photographs in this book are from the author's own collection. He would like to thank Linda Sage, Beth Easdown, Gordon Wallis, and Samantha Black (for the bottom photo on page 22). Many original documents, as well as written and online sources, have been consulted, including the following books: the Kent and London South volumes of *The Buildings of England* series, Hasted's volumes on Kent (1797–1801), Greenwood's *An Epitome of County History: Vol. 1, Kent* (1838), and *The Destruction of the Country House* (1975).

ABOUT THE AUTHOR

Martin Easdown is a well-respected Kent historian who has also written extensively about the seaside piers of the United Kingdom. His first local book, *A Grand Old Lady*, appeared in 1996 and in 1997 he produced his first joint effort with Linda Sage, *Rain, Wreck and Ruin*, which they followed up in 1998 with *The History of Spade House, Sandgate*. Their other collaborative efforts include *Folkestone under Water* (2001), *Hythe in Old Picture Postcards* (2002), *Folkestone in Old Picture Postcards* (2003), *Hythe: A History* (2004), *Foul Deeds and Suspicious Deaths Around Folkestone and Dover* (2006), *Mansion of Mirth* (2007, with Eamonn Rooney), *Hythe Through Time* (2010), and *Hythe: The Postcard Collection* (2017). In addition, Martin has produced books on Folkestone's pier (*Victoria's Golden Pier*, 1998), pubs (*Tales from the Tap Room*, 2000 and *More Tales from the Tap Room*, 2004 – both with Eamonn Rooney), and First World War air raids (*A Glint in the Sky*, 2004, and *Poignant Journey*, 2017).

Torry Hill, Milstead – built in the 1850s, but demolished in 1958 to be replaced by a new house.